GUSTAV HOLST

FOUR PART-SONGS

for unaccompanied chorus

NOVELLO PUBLISHING LIMITED

CONTENTS

NOTE

These four early and unperformed part-songs are among a number of vocal works by her father which Imogen Holst edited shortly before her death in 1984. 'O lady, leave that silken thread' was composed in 1895 (H.4 in Imogen Holst's *Thematic Catalogue of Holst's Music*); 'Soft and gently' in 1896 (H.13); 'The autumn is old' in 1899 (H.48); and 'Winter and the birds', the earliest of the four, in 1894 (H.App.1, 40).

London, 1986   *Colin Matthews*

FOUR PART-SONGS
1 O LADY, LEAVE THAT SILKEN THREAD

THOMAS HOOD

GUSTAV HOLST
(1874-1934)
edited by Imogen Holst

2 SOFT AND GENTLY

HEINE
(translator unknown)

GUSTAV HOLST
edited by Imogen Holst

3 THE AUTUMN IS OLD

THOMAS HOOD

GUSTAV HOLST
edited by Imogen Holst

10

morn-ing, Cold Win-ter gives warn-ing. The ri-vers run cold,_____ The red sun is

morn-ing, Cold Win-ter gives warn-ing. The ri-vers run cold,_____ The red sun is

morn-ing, Cold Win-ter gives warn-ing. The ri-vers run cold,_____ The red sun is

morn-ing, Cold_ Win-ter gives warn-ing. The ri-vers run cold,_____ The

14

sink - - ing, And I am grown old_____ And life is fast shrink-ing, There's e-

sink - - ing, And I am grown old_____ And life is fast shrink-ing, There's e-

sink - - ing, And I am grown old_____ And life is fast shrink-ing, There's e-

red sun is sink - ing, And I am grown old And life is fast shrink-ing, There's e-

17

- now for sad think-ing,_____ There's e - now for sad think - - ing.

- now for sad think-ing,_____ There's e - now for sad think - - ing.

- now for sad think-ing,_____ There's e - now for sad think - - ing.

- now for sad think-ing,_____ There's e - now for sad think - - ing.

4 WINTER AND THE BIRDS

FRITZ HART

GUSTAV HOLST
edited by Imogen Holst